waterways series

A Class Act

releasing new voices, revealing new perspectives

A Class Act
Poems: 2000-2015

waterways
a series of flipped eye publishing
www. flippedeye.net

First Edition

The author is grateful to Paul McMenemy, editor of the *Lunar Poetry Magazine.*
who originally commissioned this collection.

ISBN-978-1-905233-53-3

Thanks to everyone who has helped. You know who you are.

*'And to Niall O'Sullivan, for sorting and shuffling, cutting and crafting
... and much good advice. Cheers, mate.'*

A Class Act
Poems: 2000-2015

A Class Act
Poems: 2000-2015

Contents

Death of a Pie 'n Mash Shop

Real poets don't do that nine to grind,
Schlep to work on the Northern Line,
Wage slavery thing.

Real poets don't handle personal cases,
Organise strike ballots,
Or stand on picket lines.

Real poets don't wear Harringtons,
Ben Sherman button-downs,
Or step out in proper daisies.

Real poets don't rub-a-dub with
A damn fine Guyanese gal,
Inna dance at the Betsey.

Real poets don't eat pie 'n mash,
With an old china, at Clarks,
On Exmouth Market.

Not anymore they don't.

A Class Act

It's the thin veneer that's so insulting,
As if we should be grateful
That they feel the need to lie, at all.
Decisions have been taken,
Still, they are consulting their 'key stakeholders',
The ones that fall between the quite unloved unlucky
And the unfortunate but undeserving poor.

They'll play no real part in the big debate:
Why do the 'haves' need so much more to motivate them,
Whilst the 'have-nots', apparently, need so much less?
How did we get into ourselves into this sorry state?
And can we trust the ones who say
That they'll extract us from the mess?
There seems to me to be a fundamental, fatal, flaw;

A massive fault line in their master plan;
They want it both ways, want to get well
In the good times and the bad,
They want you with your head down, working for the man,
They want to stop you spotting you've been had.
Whilst those who want for nothing?
They want more.

So now we've government by clever knotting of the old school tie,
And they'll do very nicely, thank you, out of boom and bust,
So ask yourself 'what does this signify?'
Is it a nasty accident or a betrayal of trust?
The fact is, this is something that we've seen before:
This is a class act, that's what this is;
This is war.

Packaway

Pack away the nurseries into a sound-bite,
Close hospitals, turn fire stations into luxury flats.
The city alchemists have done their best
To kill the goose that laid the golden egg
But that's the beauty of it;
Base metal from the common weal can still be conjured with.
A mark is stamped upon the penny post
And pennies pinched from public sector plebs
Will reap a handsome dividend.

Deliberate denigration softens up the target,
Undermines educators.
Healers, helpers, first responders,
Are parceled up and privatised.
Infants in incubators, undergraduates,
Infirm incontinents in care homes,
Are carried off by speculators
Unencumbered by the smallest moral compass.
The profit margin is their only friend.

So pack away the nurseries, the books, the toys,
The instruments of learning and of fun,
Pack up the little girls and boys into
An education system sabotaged
And broken, quite undone,
By petty dogma, self-interest and greed.
Don't say that you weren't warned.
Unpack a future for them,
Strange and dark, indeed.

Location, Location, Location

Over-educated, under a mountain of debt,
You owe a grand for every year you've lived,
And now it's time to get back to reality,
After all those years of study,
To find a job, somewhere to live,
With friends, or shack up
With some Facebook fuck-buddy:
Going home is not an option.

II

Over the limit, under-age,
In the wee small hours, and we've reached
That stage where she's drunk herself
To death and back to life again.
Someone might get lucky,
It could just be you,
How's your father, how d'you do?
Either way we're heading for a world of pain.
Going home is not an option.

III

Over the border, under the shells,
Pinned down by small-arms fire,
And when the sergeant major
Tells them to get moving,
They do as they're told,
Take what you can carry,
Can kicked down the road,
Buy a visa with a band of gold.
Going home is not an option.

Winterreise

The roads are empty,
Now the schools have broken up,
They fly south in the winter,
Chatter of nannies and the mansion tax,
Barely keeping their heads above water,
With inky blots and rotten parchment bonds,
Barely keeping their heads above water,
Chatter of nannies and the mansion tax,
They fly south in the winter,
Now the schools have broken up,
The roads are empty.

No More Brains Than a Stone

Beautiful women ask him to but, even so,
He isn't going to vote.

The act is not political;
It's just for show.

You say you want a revolution,
Well... you know.

You've pulled, love,
Get your coat

And get your penicillin
On the NHS.

Ah, bless.
His heart's in the right place,

Not just a pretty face;
A total prick.

All trick; and very little treat;
He's landed on his feet,

Lord of Misrule,
A proper tool,

The party animals will brand him as
An ordinary fool.

And the Winner Is...

It's so cold in here,
And yet I know the ice-caps are still melting,
So here I sit and shake with fear,
Whilst next door someone's girlfriend gets a belting.

'Act local, think global' is the cry,
And though I like to think I try,
The neo-cons have got us by the balls,
As bombs go off in shopping malls,
They still can't read the writing on the walls
Of all the citadels they're storming.

It's so cold in here,
And still I know I won't turn on the heating,
At least, at last, that's one thing clear,
I'm not the one who's handing out the beating.

Live and let live, live and let die,
Though more of us are asking 'why?',
The concept of more war appalls,
Mexicans sweat, a Texan drawls,
Po' black folks cry,
Big Easy falls prey to global warming.

It's so cold in here,
They've plans to build a 'safe' nuclear reactor.
Next door he cracks another beer,
His girlfriend wipes away a tear,
She's six months pregnant with his son,
Lights up a fag, the flat screen's on,
They've voted, and they want to hear who's won...
X-Factor.

Not Good, Whatever Way You Look At It

More winter storms roll in, the rivers flood, and half of Britain's suddenly under water; blizzards sweep over America, holding that landmass in an icy grip from sea to shining sea. The deserts creep and spread, with desiccated fingers throttling Africa, whilst war and famine follow in their wake; bush fires rage across Australia, the conflagration visible from outer space. Most scientists agree a link between human activity and climate change is highly probable; our governments conclude that any action which might threaten growth is not sustainable.

The deserts creep and spread, with desiccated fingers throttling Africa, whilst war and famine follow in their wake; bush fires rage across Australia, the conflagration visible from outer space. Most scientists agree a link between human activity and climate change is highly probable; our governments conclude that any action which might threaten growth is not sustainable. More winter storms roll in, the rivers flood, and half of Britain's suddenly under water; blizzards sweep over America, holding that landmass in an icy grip from sea to shining sea.

Most scientists agree a link between human activity and climate change is highly probable; our governments conclude that any action which might threaten growth is not sustainable. More winter storms roll in, the rivers flood, and half of Britain's suddenly under water; blizzards sweep over America, holding that landmass in an icy grip from sea to shining sea. The deserts creep and spread, with desiccated fingers throttling Africa, whilst war and famine follow in their wake; bush fires rage across Australia, the conflagration visible from outer space.

What, will the line stretch out to the crack of doom?

The atmosphere is thick and heavy, humid,
Saturated, sick with syrupy sycophancy.
Obsequious drops fall heavy from the heavens,
Into the gutter, down the drain.
The thunder rolls, the guns salute,
Their lordships and their graces
Put on heirs apparent.
I can't stand the reign.

Lie Still

Lie still,
Don't move, don't blink,
Don't raise your head.
Just pray that that they don't see you breathing,
In amongst the piles of dead.

Lie, still,
Give them what they expect.
Don't flinch
As they record your answers,
All present and all incorrect.

Lie still,
Pretend to be asleep.
She's not 'in love',
He's not 'the one',
Just pray that you're not in too deep.

Lie, still,
Don't take the risk,
Don't take a breath.
This is the life,
Or, if it isn't, then it isn't death.

Shit and Flies

'The RMT train drivers' union said it would shut down Liverpool Street station on health and safety grounds if the EDL gathered there'. The Guardian – Sept. 2011

They go together just like shit and flies,
Hard times; race hate –
It's all part of the system.
The well-heeled surfers ride the wave
And skim it off the top,

We see the flash,
We feel the boom and bust,
We hear the anti-Nazi students talk about 'the fash',
Watch as the tide of hate comes rolling in,
Like a cloud of dust between tall buildings.

Between Central Office, Wapping and the Daily Mail,
The inference is that it's all in the game,
The bitterness of Britishness,
This Paki bashing by another name,
Twitter and twisted tale of bull necked, bullshit patriots.

So here we are again, three million unemployed.
Old slogans get rolled out:
'No Pasaran!', 'Not In My Name!'
We know that politicians telling lies
Are back in season.

We read about the Lawrence trial,
Step in and crack some heads,
The trains don't run on time, and for good reason.
Hard times; race hate; we've seen their kind before,
They go together just like shit and flies.

The Wide Awake Club

My old man was born in the 1920s,
During the 1940s he saw active service
With the Northamptonshire Regiment, In Italy,
Then on into France and Germany.

A little younger, my Mother (and her schoolmates)
Were evacuated to various parts of Mittel Europa,
Whilst the cities of her homeland were systematically destroyed.

After the war, with the country divided,
Half of it exchanged the tyranny of one evil dictator
For that of another.

In the second half of the century,
The nations of Western Europe began a project
To move towards a common future,
Away from the fear and hatred of the past.

Towards the end of the Millennium
The states of the Eastern Bloc
Got an opportunity to join in.

I've never had to go to war;
My nephew and niece grew up
Without the fear of death by aerial bombardment.

You kip if you want to.
Me? I'm in the wide-awake club.

The Direction of Travel

There are units of the British Army, rolling through the badlands of the Middle East In canvas sided jeeps, susceptible to snipers' bullets and to roadside bombs, although the days of building trust, soft hat patrols, of winning hearts and minds, are now long gone. Meanwhile, back in London, a variety of creeps, management consultants, media moguls, traders in bonds, gad about town in armoured 4x4s the size of bloody tanks.

So what is it that they're afraid of?

Do they fear roving bands of eco-warriors, armed with RPGs, might brew them up as they return from their demanding jobs in PR agencies and city banks? Or are they worried that their womenfolk, the lovely Lucindas, Tabithas, Samanthas, Juliets and Jades, might be ambushed, somewhere out there on the prep school run, by tank-busting crusties, hurling hand grenades, and made to pay a dreadful price for all their profligacy and insouciance?

Perhaps they should be.

It makes you wonder, when you hear the CEO of some super successful budget airline extol the benefits of climate change and cheaper air-fares in the self-same breath, if a batch of SAM2 missiles, tactically deployed, around, say, Stansted or Heathrow, might not sufficiently 'incentivise' the frequent flyers, business travelers and their ilk, to scratch the red-eye shuttle, do the decent thing and catch a train.

If they won't take the carrot, use a bigger stick.

Betrothed young lovers could well then conclude that wedding bells sound just as well in Worthing as they do in Martinique, Mauritius, or in the Seychelles. Hard-working families, making summer plans, might think travel by plane too dangerous a way to roam, the pain of endless check-in queues not worth the pleasure, and prefer to bugger off to Bognor once again.

It's either that or re-open the Millennium Dome.

What's more, next time they come to vote, they might just choose a politician who believes we should reduce demand for fossil fuels, that there is little use in shedding blood for oil, and we would all be that much safer if the troops came home.

Bread and Circuses

It's been this way since before Caesar's time,
Another leader comes, another goes.
There's never any shortage of ambitious types
And there are always those prepared
To sell out for success.
Whatever next? Who knows!
There's not much reason to it and but little rhyme.

It's been this way time immemorial:
Norman, Viking, Saxon, Roman, Celt.
Just keep your head down,
Belt up and get on with it,
We'll sink or swim together once the ice-caps melt.
They'll tell us when to worry, what to think,
In some cheap editorial.

It's been this way since time began,
They like to let us know who's boss,
They're strong on strategy, though heaven knows
They're more concerned with profit than with loss
Of freedom, whatever that means.
Few of us give a toss, the rest just hope and pray
And get away with murder, if they can.

It's been this way since before Caesar's reign:
We snap to it but they want it snappier.
Now, thanks to 'trickle down' we're that much better off,
Though inequality makes us unhappier.
They give us bread and circuses alright,
The crucifixions on the Via Appia replaced by installation art.
We're told barbarians are at the gates again.

Peasants

Our special correspondent struggles with the language. Though some might try to understand, it's hard to comprehend, it's hard to credit, that those glory-glory days in never-never land are at an end. But take a closer look: the stewards at the royal pageant are young and unemployed; unpaid; on work experience; shipped in from out of town and told to rough it on the street. Whilst the performers, asked to 'volunteer', to keep the beat at the quadrennial five ringed circus, might just identify a trend. We're being taken in. The cheering crowds, the beer and bunting, only go to show that those, so well rewarded, having ballsed it up, are going to make us pay, not once, but twice, and then again. So where's the anger? Where's the rage? What of the age-old legacy, Wat Tyler and Jack Cade? Now is the time to make or mar, not make do and mend. Hubble bubble, toil and trouble, fire burning in the rubble, bring me grief, I'll bring you double. Mark my words, my friend.

Consensus

He dropped some bangin' tunes, yeah,
But still they shivved him,
Out there on the murder Mile End road.
His shit was ill, man.
How he made it to the motor, no one knows.
The streets are silent
But the evidence remains:
A dark brown stain; glass diamonds
From the shattered windscreen; half a brick.
They talk of broken Britain;
I agree with Nick.

And she was just a baby,
When they found her, in the bathtub,
Emaciated, buggered, cut and burned.
They blamed the social workers (well, they would),
The press were outraged,
The politicians spoke of lessons learned,
Then lectured us about community,
Lied through their teeth,
And never missed a trick.
They talk of broken Britain;
I agree with Nick.

So he went for a soldier:
He smoked; he went out on patrol;
He read his mail;
He showed some backbone,
Until a sniper snapped it,
In an ambush on the Kabul trail.
And those that don't do history, well,

They won't know just when to stand and fight,
And when to get out, on the double, quick.
They talk of broken Britain;
I agree with Nick.

The bankers played the fiddle so,
Now there's hell to pay,
And fewer childcare places, youth clubs,
Hospitals and schools.
We're all in it together; take it on the chin,
Or take the voters all for bloody fools.
Cut to a consensus, a society that's 'big',
A marriage of convenience, Dave and Nick.
They talk of broken Britain
And it makes me sick.

Not Half-Empty. Drained.

The lives of others and the special demonstration unit
Come together for a money shot. She moans, then he ejaculates.
When they call 'cut', that's all we've got.

Regardless of their lordships' verdict,
We always know exactly when we're being screwed.
Some say we're stuck with it. We're not. Just super-glued.

Lectures on revolution from some hairy lecher make us yawn,
Turn off, or back to 'Strictly', else to online porn.
Tune out the Commentary on privilege, on gender, race, on
intersectionality,

'Til someone asks 'whatever happened to the working class?'
Then sigh, bend over, grasp your ankles, take it up...
With your MP.

The Hippy Chicks

Middle-aged men in Lycra dominate the traffic,
It isn't what she meant by white male privilege
But nonetheless it's true. The hippy chicks
Do yoga classes, practice meditation
And when it all gets far too, far too much for them,
They head off on retreat, in order to advance
Their skills in mindful positivity.

Emotionally intelligent, they're not concerned
By news of more nefarious activity,
As practiced by the great and good.
The hipsters, similarly sanguine,
Do just enough of nothing to get by,
Faintly ridiculous, it seems that's what they're there for,
Bless 'em, if they try they fail.

The fierce young patriots go out and put the fear of someone's god
Into some women who have chosen an identity behind the veil.
The politicians argue about matrimony, man to man,
The trickle down effect they sold us now revealed as fecal gravity.
It's a hard rain, watch it fall. They keep calm and carry on regardless,
We carry the can, suppress the rising tide of panic
In our hearts and hope the hippy chicks are proved right after all.

Peak Beard

We've reached 'peak beard', apparently.
The clever bastards having bought their shares
In razor blades. It's true, you can't put muscles on a chin
And, after all, there never was much gained by looking weird.

The bright young things are fascinated
By the pictures in the exhibition catalogue, or,
More precisely, by the smart-arse phone concealed
Behind its pages. It's all very pukka 'til some fucker rings.

Brands are reinvented on the premise
Trendsetters won't realise that it's all been done before.
They'll say we're 'haters' when we call them on it.
Lines shaved from a sonnet prove that less is more.

Artisan Flat White

So what if some limp Hampton, with a sleeve of ink, silly barnet and no use for a razor, is eating pulled-pork in-a-bun where I used to order two 'n two? It's no big deal. You can't get curry goat or dub version at the market anymore these days and good coffee is scant recompense. Artisan flat white, my arse! So, this is progress, if not the progress that we hoped to make. Don't give up.

From Ferguson to Ramallah, coming out with your hands up is no guarantee. The Big Smoke takes no prisoners but it's not Donetsk, far less Mosul or Kirkuk. Just poor doors, rough sleeper spikes, high rents and hipster bars. Keep going. Don't be afraid to contribute a verse, a punch, or an opinion. Don't give in, give out or give a shit what they think.

Don't forget your friends, or who your mates are.

Don't quit. No, don't give up, for pity's sake.

Hand Torn Edge

Do not feed the crack heads
In the low-brow areas,
It is not advisable
To flaunt your filthy lucre
Here, where you accent is desirable,
Your cover, blown.

As if change was progress,
For richer, for poorer, better or worse,
A caff closes, an estate agent
Opens for business, as well
As if a manor of thy friend's,
Or of thine own.

Bitter Man

It takes much longer to get out of the station now it's been improved,
They say that it will cut the time it takes to get from East to West
To East but we shall not be moved,
At least until they price us out of house and home.
Of course we've always had the right to roam these streets,
Until they drop the bomb we're going to drop the beats,
So drop-dead gorgeous boys and girls from out of town
Will get sucked in and then they'll get sucked down,
Just like the beer they drink that's pale and stale.
The hip-hop-heads can't keep it real,
Like they can't keep real ale.

But meanwhile in the East End there's a suede-head bard
Whilst way out West my mate fights on the undercard,
Dying to be there, some people say they wish I would,
That I should get out more, that it would do me good
But Checkpoint Charlie here is stuck at TCR,
South of the river is a bridge too far,
And I am too far gone to change my ways,
It comes to something when you're bitter,
That you can't get bitter,
In the city,
Any more these days.

Mental Mud Hut

Come the day the oil runs out,
The man accused of living in a mental mud hut
Might permit himself a small, wry smile.
He may not know exactly where he's going
But he knows that he will get there on his feet, in style.

The rhythm that he's moving to's the beating of his big old broken
heart;
This ain't no petrol driven, battery operated gig;
The pace is brisk, the melody that's playing in his head
Provided by the singing of a blackbird,
Not the insistent 'tsk, tsk, tsk' of some numpty,
With a nodipod, his brains removed by spending too long on the X-box,
Strap-hung-up on the Northern Line.

Post carbon we can all expect to live the quiet life,
Though human nature being what it is,
There's little sign the same old same old won't grab an unfair share,
The way they've always done.
Soon come, the day the oil runs out.
Meanwhile, the man accused of living in a mental mud hut
Thinks it isn't going to make much difference;
They'll still get away with murder;
He'll be the one who goes the extra mile.

I Spy

Can't do semiotics, doesn't read the signs,
Not neurotypical; not diagnosed,
Just one of those who have to
Live between the lines,
Penned in the margins,
Out in the cold, cold sweat,
Someone you dreamt of,
No-one you met.
Well versed in tradecraft,
Dead letters dropped,
Has gone the distance,
Never been stopped
At the border,
Under control,
Sleeping together,
Ratty and Mole.
Twice is coincidence,
Three times, a plot,
One is an accident,
Except that it's not that easy,
Behaviours are learned,
At deep extra cover,
An agent is turned.

The Strange Demise of the Working-Class Male

He's serious, like cancer,
He's not fucking about,
Life's not so mysterious,
He's got it all worked out,
Out brief candle,
His poor player
Merely struts and frets,
He doesn't have a prayer
And no one's taking bets
On him going the full distance,
Now he's lost his punch,
He offers some resistance
But it's all based on a hunch
That he's been playing
For more than long enough,
Now they've heard what he's saying
And they're going to call his bluff.

Tough guy though he might have been
Prepared to compromise,
He just can't keep his nose clean
And it would be unwise to trust to sentiment,
When they don't understand,
That it's not much of an argument,
If it can't be settled
With a swift right hand.

D.O.A.

Foot down on the wah-wah pedal,
Emergency response in full Doppler effect,
By the time they reach the fun's already over,
Someone's big night out already wrecked.
Blue light, black light, blue light, black light,
Blue light illuminates a pallid face,
The uniforms come in team handed,
Just in case,
Time is of the essence,
Now the race is run,
Casualty to casualty,
And there is none of this
Mucking about at red or amber,
It's straight up, over and across
The sodium glare,
Between the kerbstone and the camber
Spreads a claret stain
That wasn't there
Before the vital signs are stable
Comes a passage of indecent haste,
An empty operating table,
Little time to waste.
There are more deserving cases
For the tired triage nurse,
Who welcomes all the unfamiliar faces,
Still life, could be worse.
All these injuries are self-inflicted,
One way or another
But we shouldn't mock
Suicidal man afflicted by his brother,
Sister says we're going into shock.

They seem to sense some tension in the muscle,
Mistake it for the reflex fight for breath,
An ally in the elemental struggle,
Against the everlasting nothingness of death,
But evidence for will to live can be misleading,
How were they to know,
The very essence of a being pleading,
Please, please, please,
Just let me go.

Going Forward

There's a fine art
To boxing on the retreat,
Not everyone can throw punches,
Going backwards.

There's a real skill, you see,
In getting any power
Into the jab,
When you're in reverse gear.

Or into the long,
Straight right,
With the weight
On the back foot.

Defensive smarts,
Evasive quality,
Are underappreciated arts,
These days.

The close calls go
To those who show
They want it more,
To the judges.

You can wind up
On the wrong end
Of a bad decision,
All too easily.

No reason, though,
To lower your standards,
Or, heaven forbid, your guard.

Though lower expectations
And a realistic approach,
Come with the territory, over time.

Just make sure they have to take
One or two coming in.
Going forward.

This Boy

This boy has fast hands and a brilliant smile,
The camera loves him,
His name, his skin, his faith
Attract the politicians,
The sweat drips off the wall,
The sharks circle.
This is a bloody business,
This is the hurting game.

This boy has good friends and bad influences,
He's got problems,
His name, his skin, his faith,
Misconceived in the melting pot
Of the mighty monoculture.
The sweat drips off the wall,
The sharks circle.
This is a bloody business,
This is the hurting game.

This boy has good teeth and a bad attitude,
He's got religion,
His name, his skin, his faith
Picked up in prison,
It's a passport to paradise...
Blown to hell.
This is a bloody business,
This is the hurting game.

This boy has brilliant hands and a fast smile,
He's been on the telly.
His name, his skin, his faith

Don't seem to matter,
The people love him,
The sweat drips off the wall,
The sharks circle.
It's still a bloody business,
It's still the hurting game.

And the new...

Round six: the atmosphere in here is pretty tense; he's always started slowly and you've got to think we gave away the first three rounds tonight. It's close but there's a calm and confidence about the way he works in there so, if I had to make a call right now, I'd say he's got this fight: judging the distance, moving both head and body, doubling the jab. Look, now there's not much coming back, he's staying in the pocket, shortening that big right hand. See, I can tell, although the other kid's got heart — no doubt — he's taking some big shots and, if his corner don't get brave, they'll do the decent thing and pull him out.

We're way up in the stands, though when I turn to tell you that I think we've seen enough, and that they ought to stop it, you're not there. Of course you aren't, I came with someone else, it has been years. So, when the crowd roars, and I look back to see the new champ with the belt around his waist, the only tears are those of joy upon the faces of the pretty girls that I embrace. They say life isn't fair – but these? These are the good times. We've got ourselves a British Champion and, after all, it's not that difficult to find another 'piece of skirt'. But I'm reminded, it's the punches that you don't see coming are the ones that hurt.

Wake Up and Smell the Coffee

Life is like a race that you're in,
And the race that you're in
Is like a nightmare that you're in;
You can never go fast enough.
Life is like a race that you're in,
And the race that you're in
Is like a nightmare that you're in;
You just get slower and slower.
Life is like a race that you're in.

And the race that you're in
Is like a nightmare that you're in is like life;
You can never go fast enough.
And the race that you're in
Is like a nightmare that you're in is like life;
You just get slower and slower.
And the race that you're in
Is like a nightmare that you're in.

And the nightmare that you're in
Is like life, and life is like a race that you're in;
You can never go fast enough.
And the nightmare that you're in
Is like life, and life is like a race that you're in;
You just get slower and slower.
And the nightmare that you're in is like life.

Life is like a race that you're in,
And the race that you're in
Is like a nightmare that you're in, is like life.

The Power of Positive Thinking

I don't believe that everything will be just fine,
I don't believe that you'll always be mine,
I don't believe that everything will turn out for the best,
I don't believe that I'll feel better once I get this off my chest.

I don't believe that everything will be OK,
I don't believe a single word they say,
I don't believe that if I work hard I'll do well,
I don't believe in heaven and I don't believe in hell.

I don't believe that a new car, or a new sofa,
Or a new born babe will really make me happy,
I don't believe that I'll have missed that much
If I don't ever change a nappy.
I don't believe in long walks on the beach
With wife and kids and Labradors,
I don't believe salvation's within reach,
In life, liberty or the pursuit of laughter and applause,
Or in clutching at straws. I don't believe

That it's exciting to be fighting a lost cause,
I don't believe that life is all too brief,
I don't believe that it's too short for grief,
I don't believe that I lack self belief,
Just that I don't believe in Santa Claus.

I don't believe that it's worthwhile pretending,
I don't believe there'll be a happy ending,
I don't believe my love is worth the sending,
I don't believe. I am not expecting

That you should conceive of me
As being more than just another ranter.
I don't believe the whole wide world,
This world wide web of self-deceit we weave,

I don't believe, I am beyond belief,
Just like I don't believe,
I don't believe, I don't believe
In Santa.

Look and Learn

The charcoal skeletons of trees,
In silhouette against a pale grey sky,
Had never promised anything of spring,
Nor given guarantee that warmer weather
Ever would bring leaf green life back in again.
So how were we to know that they were dead?
That by the summer they'd be down,
By autumn stacked in neat log piles,
As winter fuel, ready to burn.

That New Year I did nothing right,
Though, smiling wanly,
Calculated longer holidays
Would do the trick,
The way they always did.
But then you changed your mind, or made it up,
Or just decided you'd leave me behind.
Too cruel, too kind,
Too late to look and learn.

Back to Nature

When they lived together
He made sure he always did
His share of household chores:
Half the laundry; half the hoovering;
Half the washing up.
Cleaning the bathroom
Let him down, of course.

Now that he's on his own,
He still does exactly half
Of what's needed to be done:
Half the laundry; half the hoovering;
Half the washing up.
The flat's returning to its natural state,
It has become a cave,
Somewhere to shelter,
Nowhere to run.

Either Way

Perhaps,
Perhaps it would be easier
If you were dead.
I do it anyway,
Behave the way you'd want me to,
If you'd been taken from me
In some sudden, tragic accident.

I hope you understand that I meant
Every word I said.
You do it anyway,
Behave the way I'd want you to,
If I were dead,
It would be easier, perhaps,
Perhaps.

Give Me No Love

Give me no love, I just can't use it,
Give me no love, I'd only abuse it,
Give me no love, I'd only lose it,
Give me no, give me no love.

Give me no such thing as society,
Give me a drink, give me sobriety,
Give me no, give me no love.
Give me a steak in this great meritocracy,
Give me a real bellyful of hypocrisy,
Give me no, give me no love.

Give me a breather, give me a break,
Give me some, give me some give and some take,
Give me the needle, give me the dope,
Give me some hope against hope against hope.
Give me asylum, give me away,
Give me a part in the play for today,
Give me no, give me no love.

Give me nowhere to run to, baby,
Give me nowhere to hide,
Give me a cause to die for,
Give me god on my side,
Give me the old, old story,
Give me the cold, hard facts,
Give me 28 days in Pentonville
For not paying the damn Poll Tax.

Give me chemical weapons,
Give me the poxy clap,

Give me more than I bargained for,
Give me less of your crap.

Give me some sense of the wider community,
Give me protection, give me immunity,
Give me no, give me no love.

Give me a nation at ease with itself,
Give me my share of the national wealth,
Give me no, give me no love.
Give me some credit, give me some cash,
Give me head, give me bed, baby, give me a bash.
Give me the carrot, give me some stick,
Give me, forgive me for being a prick.
Give me a hit, give me a miss,
Give me and take me away from all this.

Give me no love, I just can't use it,
Give me no love, I'd only confuse it,
Give me a way out I'm going to use it,
Give me no, give me no love.

Give me no love, 'cos I've had it before,
Give me no love, I don't want anymore,
Give me a window, give me a ledge,
Give me some space, now I'm close to the edge,
Give me a rush and a push and a shove,
Give me no, give me no love.

Now. Here. This.

We live in the moment,
Just at present.

Even so,
It's all too good to last.

What we have here and now
Is very pleasant.

Haunted
By the none too distant past.

The Conversation

I would like to extend the conversation.
I have enjoyed our long and late-night chats,
The discovery that we both like cats,
Books, music, poetry, share an interest in progressive politics
But I would like to extend the conversation.

I would like to extend the conversation
From a fleeting smile,
Through a meeting of minds,
To a deeper form of communication.
I would like to extend the conversation.

I would like to extend the conversation,
From the tip of my tongue,
To the nape of your neck,
To the inside of your thighs.
I would like to extend the conversation.

I would like to extend the conversation,
To the words other mouths cannot speak,
To the parts other hands cannot reach,
To the place where two bodies meet.
I would like to extend the conversation.

I would like to extend the conversation,
To the point where
We both come
To the same conclusion.

I would like to extend the conversation.

Scrabble

From across the other side of the world
She comes and she comes and she comes,
All wide-eyed smile girl, all woman,
All fingers and thumbs her nose at the negative,
The black and white and read all over,
Read all about it, baby, read between the lines.
He's hot, like a triple word score,
Awesome? Hell, yeah, lady!
And she's not judging the distance between them,
Lamenting the last of the lost days,
Or missing the push and the shove;
Just carpeing the diem,
Getting her rocks off,
Feeling the love.

North By North West

Outside the traffic thunders by on Elliot Avenue West,
Sleepless in Seattle but maybe it's all for the best,
This slightly disconnected feeling,
Where everything's familiar but nothing seems to fit,
It's a bastard when that happens on the Old Kent Road
But out here, well, who gives a shit?

Getting over and above the distance, getting close,
Got a love thing going on and baby it's the most,
The most, the most that I can do to keep from going crazy,
Though I think that I'll pull through,
Some might think these lines a little lazy
But here is one thing straight and true:
This one's not about me, lady; this one;
This one; this one's about you.

Blue on Blue

Man down in blue on blue!
It's personal. And though that's not the only bad news,
The message on the wires from across the pond
Is positive and then some.

The liberal thinkers and the democrats are cock-a-hoop;
The flat earth fascist, tea party-poopers, proper pissed off.
Over there, from sea to shining sea,
They've proved they're not so dumb.

That climate change is real;
That Darwin got it right;
That cutting taxes for the wealthy,
Only makes the richer rich.

That women, gays, Hispanics, the African Americans,
The young, the sick, the dispossessed and under-represented poor,
Sensed that the 'hopey changey thing' might yet work out
And make that stupid witch swallow her bile.

And millions more
Around the globe watched anxious that
They kept the faith, did not repudiate
The chance they took.

Anxious to see the tide of lies and threats and hatred,
Fear, fanatics and Fox News, held by the firewall,
Minnesota, Iowa and Illinois,
Ohio shook...

And held.

Whilst, on the debit side:
The House still full of bigots;
The system still corrupt;
The war continues;
The two of us agree that it is over,
We are not in love.

Hands Up, Don't Shoot

Her Pops drove a truck delivering to diners, in St Louis, through the '60s.
Well-liked, he got to eat out back with the help. White patrons only.
She knows Ferguson, went to church there growing up. Her mom
Still lives round the way. Mostly disgusted but not surprised.
The folks were never bitter and, if they were, they hid it...

Well, when we went to eat at the Chicken Shack, I felt something.
As much about accent and appetite as ethnicity. No static, no big deal.
We smiled at each other. She said Europe was different. The same,
But different. Here or there, being the 'cool black chick' was tough.
Good job, baby, and I'm glad you did it.

Blessings

Blessings don't count,
When they don't count for much,
With all the freedom in the world,
Without a loving touch.
It isn't what we have
But what we haven't got,
That fuels the fires.
It yearns me not,
Such outward things
Dwell not in my desires.
Blessings don't count,
When they don't count for much.

Not Wisely

It isn't easy, getting any credit nowadays,
Who's going to trust you with their money?
Or their heart? And there is not much love
Available to anyone who tries their best,
Who does their bit, who plays their part,
Who steps up when the shit goes down.

But if you're made that way,
Then that's the way you're made.
There are no accolades, there's little praise,
And it's a crown of thorns that's worn
By anyone who cares too much.

Life's such a bitch
But it's the dark clouds make the silver lining shine
And who would want it any other way?
Plenty! Or so it seems and so they say
That they already live in paradise;
We know that we will never reach the promised land

But we can walk a step or two together,
Shoulder to shoulder,
Heart to heart,
And hand in hand.

Mind The Gap

Between ourselves,
Between us and these four walls,
Between the lines, between the circle and the stalls,
Between heaven and a hell on earth,
Between what we get paid and what we're really worth.

Between the Sun and Moon, Between Venus and Mars,
Between the Hawksmoor churches and the girly bars,
Between here and where we want to be,
Between the wage slaves and their liberty.

Between the sheets,
Between the pimps and whores,
Between foxhole and no-man's-land,
Between the wars, between mad mullahs and the neocons,
Between what we've been told and what is really going on.

Between a rock and a hard place,
Between a fine wine and a pretty face,
Between hope and fear and love and hate,
Between the first move and... checkmate.
Between two stools, between us and them,
Between the trustafarians...
And the Yard Men, dem.

Between politicians, between right and wrong,
Between here and where we're coming from,
Between there and where we want to be,
Between our expectations and reality.

Between what we destroy and what we make,
Between the way we live our lives and what the earth can take,
Between take-off and landing, between push and shove,
Between misunderstanding... two people in love.

Between the best of friends and,
Maybe baby, between you and me...
Here's where the story ends,
Between the devil and the deep, blue, sea.

Ganz Vorbei

I never felt so very much alone,
As I did at my mother's funeral,
Though in reality, of course,
I had been on my own
For years and years and years
And years and years and
All that death had served,
By calling so unkindly,
Was to remind me of
How little time we have;
And that we don't
Outlive our fears.

All This Poetry

Nothing will change, no clocks will stop,
She'll finish breakfast, jump into the car
And drop the kid off,
Just like she's always done.
Well, at least, just like she's done
Since she stopped thinking of him as 'the one'
And found some other mug to do the dirty deed,
To get called 'daddy'.

Nothing will change, she may not even know,
And there is every reason to believe
That she would go on living,
With or without the help of Auden,
And only the odd person on the 8.05 to Morden,
Via Charing Cross, might ever mark the loss
Of that spare man, the one who always seemed so bitter,
Though they heard tell that he was fitter than a butcher's dog.

Nothing will change. Some may recall the time
He hit that chap, the one who let his litter fall,
The one who offered an unwise response to the suggestion
That he 'pick it up and put it in the bin'.
Or the fat lad, acting anti-social, making an awful din,
Who was quite surprised to find that being disrespectful,
When you're asked to turn the music down,
Can be all that it takes to get your face pushed in.

Nothing will change. It's not enough to have a go,
To do your stuff, to give it your best shot,
To do the right thing at the time
But, if that's the way it goes, well, OK, fine.

It's not so hard to understand
That if you don't deliver, as expected, on demand,
Then you will not be mourned too much by anyone,
No matter that you loved them more than life itself.

Nothing will change. Though we'd all like to think
That we'd be missed, that our loved ones
Would blink and wipe away a tear,
Recall some much-loved piece of verse,
Before the memory grows dim,
Indifference isn't that surprising,
When all you read's the Boxing News and Rising,
If you won't do the decent thing, then what do you expect?

So, though she may show some signs of distress,
Nothing will change, no clocks will stop, you'll see.
It's just that there will be a little less of all this poetry.

Thank you for buying *A Class Act*. It is Chip Hamer's first poetry collection with us; we hope you enjoyed it - we certainly did! You can find out more about Chip online.

—§—

the waterways is a contemporary poetry series of flipped eye publishing, a small publisher dedicated to publishing powerful new voices in affordable volumes. Founded in 2001, we have won awards and international recognition through our focus on publishing fiction and poetry that is clear and true, rather than exhibitionist.

If you would like more information about flipped eye publishing, please join our mailing list online at: www.flippedeye.net